I0151263

Downsizing
Before Transition

Downsizing
Before Transition

How Seniors Transition With Less
Stress, Frustration and Overwhelm

JEFF TURNER

Copyright © 2015 Published by Jeff Turner & JLT Publishing Group. Printed in the United States of America. All right reserved. No part of this book may be reproduced in any form or by electronic or mechanical means including information storage without express written consent of publisher.

Edited by Alicia Yurechko
Formatted by Gail A Henry-Walker
Cover designed by Visualarts
Distributed in the USA

JLT Publishing Group
570 Broadway PO Box 816
Amityville NY 11701

DEDICATION

Dedicated to my mother: Cassie M. Turner. I wrote this poem the day after she died from breast Cancer. Sept 26 2012.

MOM'S GONE… ON THE OTHER SIDE OF TIME!

Mom, thanks for all the things you taught me and all the years of tough love. You taught me to speak my mind without fear, and what I should do when things weren't clear.

You gave me good advice that I didn't always understand and listen to. Now I can only reflect on your advice as I meditate on it while I miss you.

You cooked our food, washed our clothes, and even made some when we were small. You taught us to stay organized it seemed like you did it all.

You made us clean our rooms and do other chores. I remember the beating you gave me and Jerry because of the poop drawings you found in the wall.

You would yell at me to get upstairs and clean my

room, which sometimes I didn't listen and understand. You knew I would need these skills as I grew up to become a man.

When I asked you for advice you didn't bite your tongue. It didn't matter if it was my two older brothers who asked, or me your baby son.

You called it like you saw it and most of the time it was true. I use to look back and wonder how you would do the things you do.

You sent us to Sunday school so we could learn about God. How in the world did you know that my life would turn out so hard?

How did you know I would need to call on the name of the Lord? Did you look into the future and see the things I couldn't afford?

It must have been hard for you as a child but you never seemed to complain. You had the wisdom that life is not about coming out of a storm but learning how to dance in the rain.

You have been such a blessing to me and this I will always share. I don't know if there's another mother out there to you I can compare.

When my friends came around and I introduced them, you would say, "shut up" and walk away. You'd have us cracking up in the midst of it all but I knew you loved us anyway.

You seemed to always believe in my dreams when others would only doubt. You would defend my stand like a trial attorney only difference you had a soft shout.

When my dream to buy a new truck for my business was close and my credit needed repair. You came through for me, you trusted in me, mother, you were right there.

Now even though the debt for that truck has been long gone and I'm sure soon I'll forget it, I'll never forget the things you taught and the love you gave, so I'll get it.

One day my hope is to see you again and to show you I made it through. But until that day, on the other side of time, I'll simply say I love you.

I love you mother!

Jeffrey

Biology is the least of what makes someone a mother.

Oprah Winfrey

CONTENTS

"First they ignore you, then they laugh at you, then they fight you, then you win."
Mahatma Gandhi

ACKNOWLEDGMENTS

First and for most I acknowledge my Lord and savior Jesus Christ who loved me enough to die for me. I've been writing for a long time. Mostly taking notes in church, seminars and meeting. I didn't discover my true love of writing until one day finding over fifty notebooks when I was moving. I am grateful to have found this true love where I can express myself freely with no interruption. This work is a fusion of my first life as a student of business and marketing, my second as an entrepreneur, and my third as an author. In a sense it is attributed to the many colleagues, clutter removal clients and people I've studied down through the year.

I got the idea for this book while attending an infusion soft conference. It was a two day training that help entrepreneurs understand more of a sales channel. I'd already been working on another book but wasn't ready to put it out. I met a gentleman that was a speaker that had a very small book about 20 lessons when speaking. I was determined before I left the conference that I would write a short book to position myself as the number one authority for seniors in transition.

I want to thank my dad for training me as a young boy with a good work ethic. My brother Jerry (my pastor) who always encourages me to live life. Thank my friend Kareem (Stork Porter) for sending books over the years when I needed them. My friend Leighton who always tells it like it is. My buddy Barry Abrams for telling me "Jeff, you got it man." My brother Joe for his encouraging spirit. My high school coach Norm Maisel who believed in me more than I could believe in myself. Perry Marshall, Dan Kennedy, Richard Koch, Richelle Shaw, Brendon Burchard, Michael Gerber, Jack Zufelt, Dale Calvert have contributed to my inspiration in sharing part of my story and message to the world.

NOTES

A cognitive disability is defined as a serious difficulty remembering, concentrating, or making decisions;

Self-care disability as difficulty bathing or dressing;

Independent living disability, with difficulty doing errands alone;

Mobility disability, a serious difficulty walking or climbing stairs;

ALARMING STATISTICS FOR THE ELDERLY IN THE US

"Dementia affects one in eight persons over the age of 65 in the United States and one in three persons over the age of 80," **Dr. Gayatri Devi, neurologist at Lenox Hill Hospital in New York City.**

INTRODUCTION

There are many transitions that we make in life starting with our birth. We transition from new born to infancy, toddlers, mid childhood, and preteen years. We reach our adolescence years and then go into early adulthood. We transition to middle age then seniors.

Transition happens through all these stages of life and it's up to us to learn the lessons so that they are smooth. We change jobs, friends, boyfriends, girlfriends, husbands and wives. We change careers, houses, apartments, cars, wardrobes and we even change our philosophy about life. When I speak on downsizing before transition I could speak on many topics including the ones I mentioned earlier. In this book we focus on seniors in the last stages of their lives.

One reality of life is that when we are too old and can no longer take care of ourselves we'll need to have someone take care of us. This can be done in the home where we reside at the time. It could be in a family member's home. It could be in a twenty four hour care facility such as a nursing home or an assisted living community. Whatever option that we choose or is chosen for us, there are steps that must be taken to ensure a smooth transition.

Most people don't think about this. Pay much attention to it or prepare for the reality that we are getting older every day. You may be getting close to this chapter of your life or you know someone that is going through it right now. You may know a care giver or you may be a care giver yourself. One thing that I've learn over the years from my expert perspective on this subject is that we all will have to deal with the stuff we've accumulated over the course of our lives. Have you ever heard the expression *you can't take it with you?* This reference is usually given when we are talking about someone dying or as some like to use passing away. But I'm here to tell you that you can't take it all with you when you're transitioning either. You must start downsizing before transition.

Have you ever wondered how the man that gets rid of your extra stuff when you're moving gets rid of your stuff? This man gives it away while creating jobs and opportunities for young people. So stop wondering! There will be many questions, concerns and much advice needed during this time. You may need to get the advice from an elder law attorney. You may need advice from an assisted living community. You may need to organize movers and downsize specialists. You may have to contact your local real estate agent to sell your property.

All of this may or may not involve family members. If it does, it can sometimes be very stressful when making decisions because sometimes you may not agree. When doing it alone, it can be extremely overwhelming with all the decisions you must make and all the options and work that needs to be done.

My advice is to seek wise council and get as much expert help that will do the physical work as possible. If you're working with family members, assign the most organized person to head the project and delegate tasks. Someone may do research for the task, another may be the one that talks to the professionals. Another may help with packing for the move.

Downsizing before transition gives real life stories of real people who had to transition, helps in transitions and become care takers. It will help you create a plan of action to the best of your ability. It will give you references, resources, and helps you move forward with less stress and frustration with the task at hand. Hopefully it helps you understand that we all go through this reality.

You may be without family members to give you a hand. Don't get bent out of shape or upset about it. You can get through it and it will not last forever.

Remember this too shall pass while you're going through it and an attitude of gratitude will help you through. Be grateful for the opportunity to serve your family member in need because one day you may need the same help.

ALARMING STATISTICS FOR THE ELDERLY IN THE US

"Nearly 70 percent of people who reach age 65 ultimately will need some form of long-term care."
The Health and Human Services Department

CHAPTER ONE

CHAPTER'S OF OUR LIVES... I ONCE WAS YOUNG AND NOW I AM OLD

Everyone has a story and just like a book there are chapters in our lives. There are chapters in the beginning, middle, and end. In the beginning we are born and first see our parents. When we move closer to the end we can no longer take care of ourselves and have to move. In the middle of these chapters people come and go. Have you ever asked this question? Why do people come and go in and out of our lives? Can you relate to some of these situations? "My first girlfriend, Dana, died suddenly of Lupus in high school. I was seventeen years old. My grandmother passed when I was twenty two." "My daughter's mom walked out of my life two years after my first daughter Syreeta, was born. I was twenty four." "My best friend at the time Dumar, was murdered. I was twenty six. Another good friend, Larry, was shot dead. I was twenty eight." "Plenty mentors and others who've had major impacts on my life have come and gone out of my life." These things happen to everyone, but not exactly the same.

Our life's like a chapter book

"My oldest sister, Cathy, died when I was thirty nine." "My wife left walked out of my life at age forty two." "My mom died when I was forty six, due to a stroke. She'd been battling breast cancer for over five years." I'm sure people have come and gone out of your lives, to many to name. One consistent thing that I see in every individual's life story is that it reads just like a chapter book. There's a beginning, middle and an end.

When people come in our lives, a chapter opens and when they leave that chapter ends. Some books are shorter, some are longer. As we get older, the pages turn; a chapter begins and another chapter ends, in this process called the book of life we all flip through. Things change, that's part of life; we start young and become old, that's part of life. Another page turns, another chapter finishes, but life continues to move on just like a chapter book until the end!

ALARMING STATISTICS FOR THE ELDERLY IN THE US

"The private sector is developing new housing options, technologies and services in recognition of the potential market for assisting older adults with aging in the community."
Harvard Joint Center for Housing Studies

CHAPTER TWO

SMOOTH TRANSITION

One Move To The Next

We all have to transition through a period of life. Nobody's transition is exactly the same and we transition even when we are getting older. One way to make the transition as smooth as possible is to accept it. I've learn this lesson well in just under a half century. "I'll be fifty years old next year and I've moved over forty five times in my life. So I know a whole lot about transitioning and downsizing personally." My friend, Leighton, always tells me that he doesn't know anybody like me. He says, "You transition better than anybody that I know." I try not to resist change anymore when I can't change it.

A lot of people resist changes and it makes it that much harder. I've learned to embrace change because there is usually better coming. I guess you can call me a personal transition expert. A few years ago, I started a junk removal company helping people get rid of their junk. I've been studying business and marketing for over thirty years and I noticed that the industry was growing, but I needed to be different.

At the time, I was going through something in my personal life and, to make a long story short, my wife left me for the second time. It really hurt, but I had to make the transition. Around the same time Kareem, a friend of mine, sent me a book in the mail by Dan Kennedy called "The Ultimate Marketing Plan." Dan said, "If you're in an industry and want to dominate a market you should write a book." That was the first time I ever heard any marketing guru teach this. Little did I know that Dan's book would create another turning point in my life after a major transition! This book would be a book I promise my mom that I would finish and dedicate to her while she was on her death bed. You never know what will change the direction of your life so keep your eyes open.

Hopefully, here you may see that change. I want to get you thinking to prepare for life's changes so you create smooth transition. If you're not aware of what goes on in the lives of seniors and their caretakers the stories in the coming chapters will help. These stories have impacted seniors, care takers and many businesses around them. The stories will continue to grow as time passes and the elderly get older.

ALARMING STATISTICS FOR THE ELDERLY IN THE US

"Among individuals aged 80 and over, more than three-quarters live in their own homes."
AARP Foundation

CHAPTER THREE

Jeffrey, Get Upstairs and Clean Your Room!
Cassie Turner

"LOOK MOM I FINALLY CLEANED MY ROOM

Before ideas are born, the seeds take time to develop in the womb of your mind. While it's being developed, nobody can see it! Around the same time my first book idea was conceived, I was moving again. I found over fifty notebooks that I had written in over the years. I realized that writing was one thing that I loved to do. I also loved to tell stories and teach, so this was the perfect way to get my message out. So I started writing a book about my life, and

13

how so much clutter affected me in every area of my life. I look back now and see it was part of the therapy that helped me go through the break up in my marriage.

I was in the back yard of my mom and dad's house at the time when the title of the book came to me. Mom would always yell when I was a kid, "Jeffrey, get upstairs and clean your room." So since I was in the process of getting my life in order after my wife left me, I titled the book, "Look Mom, I Finally Cleaned My Room!"

This title was a metaphor relating to cleaning up my life. The same process mom taught me to do when she made me cleanup my room. "Look mom, I finally cleaned my room" is about dealing with junk and clutter physically but also mentally, emotionally, spiritually and in every area of our lives.

Too much clutter lead to stress

This came to me while writing the manuscript of my first book. I continued to think about my life and how out of order it was. I was stressed and depressed and started going to the track to talk to God about my situation. I met a young lady at the track that recently started a cleaning and organizing business. I told her about what I was going through and she said, "You should clean out your closets." She came to my apartment and helped me clean, get rid of some stuff in my closets, and get organized.

The funny thing was that I started feeling better. The stress and depression started to leave. Then I started doing some research about clutter and how it causes stress, anxiety, depression, children behavioral problems and even weight gain. I got my motivation back after getting rid of the junk in my cluttered closets, and the research showed that it was because of the de-cluttering. After the research, I decided to educate the public about clutter. I read in Joe Polishes newsletter about how he helps his clients create consumer awareness guides.

I've always jumped from one project to the next. So while I was writing the manuscript for my book, "Look Mom I Finally Cleaned My Room!" I created the consumers awareness guide to the dangers of clutter. I figured that I could write a small booklet that wouldn't take long. I said to myself, "I could use it to start teaching about the effects of junk and clutter not only physically but mentally, emotionally, spiritually and in our relationships." So here I was again focused on writing while doing everything else in my business.

Don't own so much clutter that you will be relieved if your house burns down.

Wendell Berry

CHAPTER FOUR

THE DANGERS OF CLUTTER

I wrote, *The Consumers Awareness Guide to: "The Dangers of Clutter!"* and its link to stress, anxiety, depression, children behavioral problems, not to mention being fat, but after writing this report I printed up about 500 hundred booklets then let them sit in my office. Why? For no other reason but the clutter of ideas I had in my head. I didn't have a team to delegate and help me implement. Having too much of anything affects us in every area of our lives. And seniors that have been living in the same place longer than most of us accumulate clutter. Some of their clutter is good and some of it is junk. But it causes dangerous situations that they are unaware of.

That's one reason I believe this consumer awareness guide should be in every home and office in America. Awareness is half the battle for change. If we are not aware that we have a problem, we won't make any changes. We can think positive about the problem but that won't change it from being a problem. We have to make a conscious or unconscious decision to change it.

That was the main reason why I created this guide to create awareness of the dangers of clutter. I told you that I love to write. At the time I was also writing articles. I noticed how a lot of people make a big deal when others have huge problems. The subject of hoarding came up and I thought to myself, everyone's a hoarder. So I wrote an article "Everyone's a hoarder; some are just more extreme!"

What I mean by this is that we all have too much stuff, more or less. And if we let go of it we'd function 100% better in every area of our lives. While going through my transitions in business and life, I've always read different books. At the time, I was reading a book called, *The 80/20 Principle* by author Richard Koch. I'd been studying the principle for over ten years. The premise of the principle is getting more from doing less.

Getting rid of eighty percent of our stuff to be more effective, happy and fulfilled in our lives is something we should really ponder. One day I decided to test the principle out in my junk removal business. I stopped eighty percent of the things I was doing and concentrated on the twenty percent of things that would make the most difference.

After four months in business we were doing more revenue in a month than I've done in a year on any job I've had. After seeing this work first hand for two years, I knew that part of my mission in life was to get people to understand this concept of "Less is more" and using the 80/20 principle would be my guide.

Having too much clutter is the perfect example of more with less when you get rid of clutter. It makes you feel better about your space including yourself. You may not understand it, but getting rid of clutter affect you in every area of your life.

Most people don't get rid of clutter because it's a habit to hold onto stuff. And habits are hard to break unless we really want to break them. It starts with awareness, so here I am creating that awareness. I teach from the philosophy of starting with subtraction when trying to accomplish anything. Elimination is the first thing we should do so that we can see things clearly.

We can be in a relationship that's not working or trying to lose weight. The few things if we ponder our situation that we can let go of make things flow better. If you've ever moved, you realize through experience how much clutter hold onto. When we move, will keep some and get rid of some. When you think about it, you see it's a huge responsibility. We have to make many decisions in a short period of time. Decision we've been putting off for years for some and from year to year for others. If it's not helping you, it's hurting you.

ALARMING STATISTICS FOR THE ELDERLY IN THE US

Elderly adults who live in nursing homes may commonly deal with aggressive or inappropriate behavior from fellow residents."
Weill Cornell Medical College in New York City

CHAPTER FIVE

MY TRANSITION TO
HELPING SENIORS TRANSITION

When I first started my junk removal company I was just like all the other companies. But after two years of massive growth, I'd stopped all my advertising and downsized my team. Why? Because our revenue was almost $40,000 a month and we were still just breaking even. I heard a comment from Dan Kennedy, who said "If you're not tracking your marketing you're wasting your time." Well, I wasn't and I stopped all my advertising at the time. I'd been drifting in my business for about seven years with stagnant sales. I was more focused on writing my books, articles, studying, creating working procedures, and creating a positioning strategy for my business. Most of all I thought about how to create my job creation platform for young people. My motivation for the business was gone and I knew I had to start doing things differently.

I'd moved about nine times within those seven years. Most recently, I moved into a nice apartment across the street from my mom and dad's house where I grew up. I was there for two years and since business was down, I fell two months behind on my rent. I was on a month to month lease and didn't know how I would catch up on my rent. So I decided to move from my $1500 a month one bedroom. I moved into a small $300 a month 7x7 finished back porch. It was the back porch at one of my employee's house. I slept in a recliner chair for four months with no TV or internet. My kids couldn't stay with me for the weekend. But, I needed to sacrifice to catch up on bills, save money and get my business back on track. The porch had room for a dresser, recliner chair, an Ikea cabinet, a microwave and a small refrigerator. I hung a closet bar up across the room and my clothes hit my head when I sat in the chair. I decreased my expenses as much as possible so that I could focus on my writing and my positioning strategy. At the same time my lap top crashed with all my documents, working procedures, articles, plans and manuscript for my book. I didn't have it backed up and I thought that I'd lost it all but I wasn't upset. I knew from past experiences that every time I lost something, some breakthrough information or concept was coming my way.

Then I came across a principle called the star principle, and it would change the way I did business forever. Perry Marshall talked about it as I sat in my recliner on the porch reading his monthly newsletters. I sat and read through the entire newsletter. Then he explained how he'd been hanging out with Richard Koch.

Richard was worth more than two hundred forty million dollars. He'd built this wealth over twenty years using his experience as a consultant and his main strategy was the star principle. Richard is the guy that wrote the 80/20 principle. Richard, said, "The number one companies in the world are there because of two main positioning strategies and these two only. They were in an industry that was growing by at least ten percent or more a year, they were first in their industry, and if you're not number one, create a new category and claim the number one spot." That's when I remembered a book I was studying in the year 2000 called, 'Focus; the future of your company depends on it.'

Al Ries and Jack Trout positioning experts said, "If you're in an industry that is overcrowded, you should narrow your focus, create a new category and claim the number one spot." I'd done it before in the landscaping industry in 2001. I went from a general landscaper working for my brother to the first specialist focused on pruning shrubs and hedges. I would use the same strategy for my junk removal company.

I'd been trying to compete with the large junk removal companies and I was doing everything they were doing. I decided I wanted to focus on seniors in transition. We wouldn't compete on price but our uniqueness and specialty. We stopped calling everything junk and started calling it clutter. Instead of using dump trucks to get rid of the clutter we would use box trucks. Why? So we could save, recycle, donate and reuse it.

Reading Richards book, 'the star principle' helped bring a lot of the concepts, principles, and strategies that I learned over the years together. It cemented the concept I learned about carving out a position that was first, unique and different. I know that others will copy us but that is a good thing. The star principle made me understand how valuable the 80/20 principle is. It brought back to mind that focusing on a specific target customer or client and their unique needs would help us create a position in our market and focus in our business.

I've come to understand over the years that seniors are sensitive about their stuff. But I wasn't fully using it to benefit them. Now I can. We're sensitive to our senior clients in many ways that our competition can't be because of their business model. When you throw good stuff in a dump truck or dumpster there is nothing sensitive about that. By understanding that seniors really cared about their stuff, we knew they would like others to use it.

This is recycling at its best. This is a sensitive time in senior's lives and it's important to be friendly, nice and are genuinely concerned. It's almost like we've known some of our clients all their lives. If you're a senior and you're in transition or you know a senior in transition you can make a difference. You are indirectly helping us support our dream, vision, mission and purpose of transforming young people lives with the stuff you're getting rid of. We recycle stuff into job training.

One in eight Americans over age 65, and nearly one in two over age 85 have Alzheimer's

AARP

CHAPTER SIX

AUNT MARIANNE FORGOT
WHERE SHE LIVED

Time for my aunts transition

My Aunt, Marianne Turner, was a part time actress in the early seventies. She's been in movies such as Shaft's Big Score and the Great White Hope. She was also a language teacher who taught foreigners English. I remember getting a birthday card from her every year when I was a kid. But such as life, time goes on and we get old. Dad had been going in and out of the city for a few days. He said, "Your Aunt Marianne is losing her memory and I'm getting nervous." Each time he would visit he would go through her things to prepare for her move.

Searching for personal paper work and other important things takes time and patients. He didn't tell Aunt Marianne what he was doing. He saw that she'd gotten to the point where she couldn't take care of herself anymore. Her bathtub was full of clothes. She wasn't cooking anymore. He knew she wasn't eating right. She would leave the building to go across the street to Dunkin Donut and stay for hours at a time. She would forget that she lived across the street.

Dad didn't feel comfortable with her living alone anymore. He'd been driving back and forth to the city for a few weeks seeing Aunt Marianne and going through stuff alone. It was time for her transition so she could be under twenty four hour care. So he decided to move her out to Long Island into a nursing home in Smithtown.

Dad called me one day and said, "I'm going into the city to move your Aunt Marianne's stuff out of her apartment." "I'll come out and help you," I said. He said, "She doesn't have much stuff, I just have to go through a little more then I will dump it all in the dumpster." Being in the business of cleaning out houses and apartments for seniors, I knew that it was more work than my dad could handle.

I knew that he couldn't do all that work on his own, but most of his life he's done things on his own and doesn't ask for help. My Aunt was 81 and my dad was 73 at the time. Even though he is still actively working, I insisted on coming out to give him a hand. Two are better than one. I couldn't see myself allowing my dad to do it alone. It was a good thing that I did come out to help because it took us about six hours to clean out that small apartment. Dad was going through things and I was packing things up and taking it down the elevator to the loading dock area. I left the good stuff in an area they designated so other people could take it if they wanted it.

The rest of the garbage I was able to throw into the dumpster. There was another area in the elevator room where I left books, plates and other small Nick Knack's for others to take. It was a slow process because it was only the two of us, but we did it. It was more like a four man job. It takes more time going up and down and elevator.

I went to visit Aunt Marianne the other day and I asked her, "Do you know who I am?" She said, "Jeffrey." She remembered me but she kept asking about my mother who passed a few years ago. I told her that my mother and Aunt Goodness, had passed and she kept asking how they were doing. She asked about four times so I know that she is losing her memory and dad made the right decision. Aunt Marianne even asked if I wanted to go visit her mother and her mother has been gone for years. I asked Aunt Marianne if she would mind if I wrote about her in my book and she said she didn't. Many seniors are getting up in age. Some have Alzheimer's and can't care for them self anymore so they need help. Dad made the decision quickly which will be hard for most people. Think about what's best for the senior and you won't have a problem making right decision sooner rather than later.

Dad and Aunt Marianne

Among individuals aged 80 and over, more than three-quarters live in their own homes.
AARP Foundation

CHAPTER SEVEN

MOM FELL… SHE CAN'T TAKE CARE OF HERSELF ANYMORE

Jackie called her sister, Susan, from Florida and asked, "How's mom doing?"

Susan said, "She's not doing well! She fell again. She can't take care of herself anymore, and we're going to have to come up with a plan to care for mom soon."

"I've been looking into a few assisted living places; I think that might be the best solution for us, but they are quite expensive. With me and Mike, working full time, we won't be able to take care of mom alone."

What options do we have with our elder parents?

"We thought about bringing her home and hiring a home health aide to come in a few hours a day, but that may not be enough."

"We also thought about the option of mom taking out a reverse mortgage to handle the cost of the assisted living community."

"I've contacted an elder law attorney to discuss setting up a power of attorney and how to handle her financials and the best way to structure mom's estate."

"Jackie, mom has so much stuff that she's accumulated over the years that has to be gone through. Maybe you can come up for a week or so once we have a plan in place to help go through some of mom's stuff."

"Just let me know," Jackie said, "and I'll put in for some vacation time."

"I've also looked up a few companies that may help with the move, called senior move managers."

"They help out families in situations like this to manage the move for seniors."

"They're located all over the country, and I spoke to a few in Long Island, so it may be a good option for us

~∝~

NASMM

There is a national association of senior move managers. They have over 800 members and growing all over the country that can help with seniors in transition. "I'm thinking we can donate what we can, but whatever they won't take, we may have to throw out because it will be a major downsize for mom" said Susan.

Susan tells Jackie that their mom really doesn't want to move, but they have no other choice. "She can't stay in her house alone for another year, because it's too dangerous. I'll start going through her important papers and put them away so that we can start the process." "After we decide what the best option is, we can set up some time to meet with a few people to handle the things that need to be done."

~∝~

Have you discussed the subject of your elder parents yet?

"I don't know why the subject of mom taking care of herself has never come up with the family, but we have to take care of it now."

"My friend Jan, had to go through the same thing last year with her mom and it was a disaster."

"She said, it took about a month just to clean out

the house because her mom held onto so much stuff. They did everything themselves, and it was so stressful and frustrating." She explained, "It was frustrating for her, Jim and her mom."

This is a common conversation today that goes unnoticed, but is a growing trend in America and even though I haven't done the research I'm pretty sure all over the world.

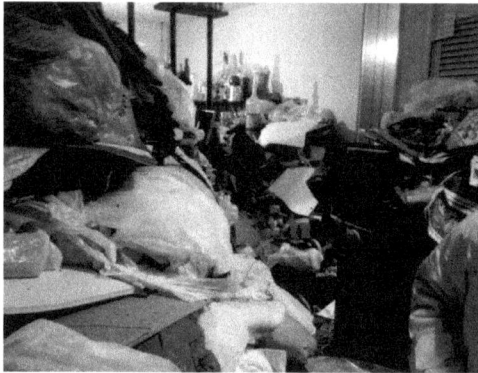

Too much clutter to get rid of

Life is one big transition!
WILLIE STARGELL

CHAPTER EIGHT

IMAGINE HOW SENIORS FEEL WHEN THEY HAVE NO CHOICE TO TRANSITION

Seniors feel overwhelm when moving

"I just feel so overwhelmed right now," Mrs. Jones, said as we cleaned out the remaining stuff out of her condo apartment in Rockville Centre. "I moved here to be closer to my niece and now that I'm selling the place my niece won't even talk to me," she said. She moved from Whitestone paying $2000 a month, to Rockville Centre paying $4000 a month, but could no longer afford it. She was having a hard time taking care of herself, so she decided to move into an assisted living community.

More and more elderly are in similar positions. To add to these burdens is not being able to handle all the stuff they've accumulated over the years now that they are moving. This is not just common with older adults, but with many people in general, and it can become very overwhelming.

Stress is commonly found in situations like Mrs. Jones's. Moving is an overwhelming feeling that can cause many other emotions, even after hiring help from a professional. Our senior population experiences more stress than others. They are usually in their homes longer, and it's really a significant, emotional change. Seniors are also set in their ways. You can't teach an old dog new tricks.

Living independently all their adult lives and then having to revert back to depend on others is a major change. Let's face it; life is a challenge no matter what we have to deal with and moving just adds to these challenges. When seniors have to move and then deal with so many things at one time, it is very stressful.

~~~

What going to happen to my stuff?

It seems like common sense to get rid of things that are cluttering up our space. But if you look up some statistics, they tell a different story. "About eighty percent of people dread de-cluttering, and one in ten hate it so much they'd rather get a tooth pulled," according to a survey of more than eight thousand Listia users in August and September 2014.

When seniors are moving, there is also the fact of what is going to happen to the stuff they've had for years. "Most people would like to know their stuff is going to good use." There are many services that will take donations, but they are very picky because they want to sell it. If the stuff is not in very good condition, it will take up space in their warehouse and cost them time and money. Sometimes the furniture is too heavy for them to take out of the house and is not worth their time to come and pick it up.

Assisted downsizing for senior's

"Our expertise is in assisting seniors when downsizing!" Our clutter removal company specializes in the new category of the junk removal industry called, "Assisted Downsizing." This new category will continue to grow at more than ten percent a year because of the aging population. One thing we do is make sure the good stuff finds a happy home.

Our slogan "Senior's Transition with Less Stress, Frustration and Overwhelm." We have a waiting list of people in need. When we find them we give furniture away at no charge if they can't afford to buy it.

When I first started the company, I would cringe

at the fact that our team was dumping so much good stuff. Now, in addition to giving stuff away for free, we also donate as much as possible to local churches that support the local community. We allow young people to use their imaginations and creativity to make other unique items with the stuff we pick up.

We're constantly looking for innovative ways to use everything that we pick up to give back to people in need and create opportunities for others. We believe in recycling and reusing, and this not only helps keep more stuff out of landfills but as I'll continue to mentioned create jobs for young people. Join our mission to impact young people's lives. We don't depend on the government but we use clutter. If you're in an organization and have an innovative way that you create with clutter let us know. We'll be more than happy to sit down and see how we can work together.

~⟋~

Create an impact with clutter

Imagine being able to use other people's clutter to create jobs. "I've waited eleven years to get my message out about my dream, vision, mission and purpose of impacting the lives of young people." It's funded by our company and some of the stuff we recycle & sell. I believe that our government is already in enough financial strain.

It will take small businesses to step up, use the

resources it has and continue to innovate to create for young people. Our children are our future and we need to invest in them. I call this concept, recycling to create jobs. In our network we teach young people to use technology and create their own jobs and opportunities. They are a big part in growing our company.

Our young people will visit the elderly that have gone into assisted living and nursing homes as well. We'll teach them that just like their needs are important older people's needs are important. It's good to donate your time to see about others. Our main mission is to make a difference in the lives of people. This makes our clients feel good. Everyone that we help downsize by getting rid of clutter, plays an indirect role in creating an impact in the lives of young people and those in need. As seniors move to the next chapters in their lives, they can feel a sense of purpose. The stuff they've accumulated and stored over the years has been stored up for this time to regenerate a new generation that has been waiting to be recharged.

Clutter in the basement

With the aging of the large baby-boom generation and increased longevity, the 50-and-over population is projected to increase about 20 percent by 2030, to 132 million.

Harvard Joint Center for Housing Studies and AARP Foundation

CHAPTER NINE

NO CHILDREN TO HELP
WITH THE MOVE

Mrs. Jones didn't have any children to move in with. Her husband passed away many years ago, so she was alone, until she decided to sell her condo. Even though her niece didn't live with her, she lived close by. But then the tables turned and brought out another side of her niece. When it comes down to money, you never know how a person will change at the drop of a dime.

Today, many people have so many time constraints because of money. They don't have the time to move parents in because they feel they are too busy. They also feel it may interfere with their normal routines and they are right. It's a huge commitment that you must be prepared for. Even though Mrs. Jones was still getting around on her own very well, she decided to sell her condo and get help like thousands of other seniors each year and growing. Assisted living communities have been popping up all over the country for the last ten to fifteen years.

It used to be that the families of seniors would take care of them. But with the growing economy and the transformation of the American culture it seems to be more convenient to have others take care of our loved ones. We have become a generation of work first and have others take care of the kids and older folks in the family. As our economy develops, it has become more focused on money and objects, rather than people and family. We are not focused on what is really valuable and important in our country just our own personal economy. For some, it is a good choice to allow someone else to care for the elderly. For others, they take on this responsibility.

As I was writing this book, I learned that the Chinese economy just took over the number one world spot that we've held since Hoover. This will be an interesting change that will affect us all. As for the baby boomers, they will need plenty of help transitioning their parents as they get older and aren't able to continue to care for themselves.

This growing adult population is in the process of transitioning from their homes to nursing homes, assisted living communities, or in with their adult children. This trend will continue for a long time. This population is growing in response to the baby boomers now starting to reach retirement age. Their aging parents are becoming of age where some need assistance.

One option is to stay home and have in home care, but the homes must be modified. There are plenty modification services that can help make the changes. Another option is to leave and move in with adult children. Even then, some things may have to be modified, or they move into assisted living communities or nursing homes.

They are designed to give 24 hour care for the elderly, but you should be careful which place you choose. You may have heard stories of seniors being abused because it's real. Either option requires plenty of thought and research.

Downsizing may require professional help. Even when the children will be handling everything, this can be an overwhelming challenge for children of elderly parents. There are services out there that can help in this process, so do your research.

~~~

Hiring a senior moving manager

For Mrs. Jones, it was a very emotional thing, especially handling it on her own. She had a company that is part of the growing community of senior moving managers come in to give her a hand. These specialized managers perform packing and organizing services. They arrange for movers, cleaning teams, junk and clutter removal teams. Assisting during this very emotional time when nobody else is around to comfort and encourage is part of the service they provide.

"Senior moving managers make the transition as simple and painless as possible." So it is a good idea to look into their help because they will save a lot of stress, frustration and overwhelm on both part of the senior parents and their children. It may be costly, but it may be well worth the cost to get the help rather than depending on friends and family. Always remember you get what you pay for. Like my good friend Leighton's elderly dad always told him, "You either pay now or you pay later, but either way you're going to pay."

*Nearly 70 percent of people who reach age 65 ultimately will
need some form of long-term care.*

The Health and Human Services Department

CHAPTER TEN

PERSONAL CAREGIVERS

I touched on an option earlier about personal caregivers. There are lots of personal care givers in all different situations. "After thirty years, my friend Leighton finally moved his father back into the family home a few years back." The first time he told me about it, I wrote an article entitled, 'Dad's moving back home.' "Even though his father is still pretty much independent, he really makes a mess of his room and the house when eating."

Leighton said it happens all the time. It's just like becoming a child all over again. In fact, his father often uses this quote, "Once a man, twice a child."

Leighton often smiles when he hears his father use this quote, because he knows how true it is!

We don't often think of our retirement years and how we will spend them while we are young. But one thing is guaranteed that it's coming for everyone that continues to live long enough. My friend understands this very well, while he's the main caregiver for his dad who is still getting around well at eighty two.

Leighton drives his dad around on errands and to the doctors on Saturday's. He says it's a tough job being a caretaker, and it will only get tougher as time goes on. He knows that one day his dad won't be getting around like he once was, and he'll have to make another decision for his dad's care.

Another good friend, Barry, has the job of a caregiver for his mom. It's a fulltime job, but someone has to do it. He picks up medicine, groceries and helps around the house. He makes sure her clothes are washed and that she's clean as well. He's been taking care of his mom ever since his dad passed a few years back.

He said, "Jeff I took care of my dad when he became ill with cancer also. Man, it was hard seeing him like that and taking care of him but who else was going to do it?" Barry, a professional speaker depleted most of his savings while taking care of his mom and dad. He told me that he almost lost the family home at one time. You never know what a person has to go through, unless you walk in their shoes.

These two friends are just two that I personally

know that have become part of the growing care givers population. This population takes care of their elderly parents, and deals with many things that most people are unaware of. It really takes a special person to handle this job, and it's going on all over the country right under our noses.

These situations sometimes cause frustration and even depression. Sometimes, the caregiver forgets to care for their own health and wellbeing because of the constant thought of the elderly parent on their mind. Care givers actually need caring and counseling, but are unaware that they need it.

Most are even unaware that they are not alone, and that there are groups out there to help them through. When caring for a loved one there is a tendency to feel that you are isolated with hardly anyone to talk to, and that no one else understands.

Recently I've joined AARP, and they have over 37 million members nationwide that use their resources and information. This is a good illustration of the growing number of seniors in this country that need help in many areas. I'm committed to using my experiences, research, and expertise to help seniors in these areas of their lives. Moving can be very emotional for seniors, so part of our mission is to eliminate frustration by sharing resources. Caring for senior's in transition and after is a full time job.

"Be the change you wish to see in the world."
Mahatma Gandhi

CHAPTER ELEVEN

HOW TO DEAL WITH EMOTIONS
WHEN YOU'RE MOVING

As for Mrs. Jones, her time was at hand and she's learning how to deal with her transition. She told me that her niece was upset because she thought that she was going to leave the condo to her and her husband. But Mrs. Jones said, "I need the money to take care of myself for the next chapter in my life."

I talked to Mrs. Jones for about thirty five minutes after finishing the cleanout and she told me her story. I don't know what situation was worse, her niece, moving, or doubling her living expenses. I tried to comfort her as much as possible and let her know that she needed to trust God through the process.

~~~

Sometimes goodbye is hard

Saying goodbye to the things we own can be a hard thing to do and very stressful, but holding onto it is more stressful. We just don't fully understand the complications. As for my conversation with Mrs. Jones, it was a very touching situation for me. I'm glad I had the opportunity to experience it with her. She was very appreciative and started to cry as she closed the door. It saddened me as she closed the door. I knew that I probably would never see her again.

It seemed that she just wanted someone to talk to. I wish I could've talked for a few hours with her, but all good things must come to an end. I'm glad I have the opportunity to talk to people when I meet them, because you never know what a person is dealing with. Sometimes just a listening ear is what they need to help them through their situation.

~~~

Over One-Fourth of U.S. Households Have a Clutter Problem
SpareFoot Survey

SpareFoot is the world's largest online marketplace for consumers to find and reserve

self-storage units, with comparison shopping tools that show real-time availability and exclusive deals. This fun tech startup is headquartered in Austin, TX.

Mentioning Sparefoot reminds of another one of our clients that was in transition. Mrs. Sands was another woman that was elderly and had to get rid of a lot of stuff.

"I'm finally getting rid of this stuff because I can't afford it anymore." Mrs. Sands, had had enough! She was paying $1000 a month for her four storage units and another $1500 a month for her condo. She said if she can clear it out, she would move in with her boyfriend who was 85 years old, and living in the same condo apartment complex she lived.

Start With Subtraction

Nevertheless, she made up in her mind that she was no longer going to spend $1000 a month for another ten years. That's over $120,000 dollars on storage fees just because she didn't want to let things go. Are you starting to see how expensive it is to hold onto stuff, especially when moving while you don't have enough space?

People hold onto good stuff but they also hold onto junk. We call the good stuff clutter, because it's most likely too much to hold onto, especially if you haven't used it in years. The stuff clutters up our space, our minds, and creates all types of stress, anxiety, and depression.

For this one reason I say that Success Starts with Subtraction! We should eliminate whatever's wasting our time, energy and space in order to be more successful in whatever we are doing. Mrs. Sand's storage units was three quarters papers. Imagine spending $120,000 to store paper. After ten years, how would that make you feel?

Everyone needs to downsize we're oversaturated with stuff

Mom's simple successful secret… Get rid of the clutter
Jeff Turner

CHAPTER TWELVE

LET IT GO: FIRST STEP TO A SMOOTHER DOWNSIZE

There is a secret to success that we are not taught in school. This secret was first revealed to me as a young boy by my mother. Sometimes, things are so simple that a person looks at it and says, "It can't be that simple because if it was, somebody would be doing it already." There are plenty of people that have discovered it and are doing it but the masses of people do the opposite. We are trained as children to have more and want more!

A common story today is that having more stuff is better especially because most of society is focused on money and what we want. We are programmed to think the more stuff we have, the more we feel important and the more successful we are. We get so caught up in the idea achieving more that we forget about what defines our happiness.

Our necessities like food, shelter and clothing usually determine our happiness, along with good relationships with friends and family. Family and deep fulfilling relationships are not at the top of many people's priority list. One thing I notice as we get older is our priorities start to change.

As I started to get older, I figured out that to be successful I needed to start by getting rid of personal belongings I didn't need. I finally understood what my mother was trying to drill in me as a boy. It was a huge awakening for me, but it took time to get it from my head to my heart. I took a while to apply it in my life for success. Sometimes, it's a huge challenge to get rid of things until we truly understand that this is the real secret to success. When you lack understanding, you hold onto things out of ignorance. You think subconsciously that you need it or that it is good for you. You don't realize that it holds you back from important decisions, opportunities and other blessings that are waiting to come into your life. My mom's important lesson when I was a boy took me forty years to understand. And it came after starting a junk removal business. Thankfully you don't have to start one, but it's up to you to understand and use this information. You just have to make a decision to get rid of the extra stuff now because it will change your life.

"You need to spend time crawling alone through shadows to truly appreciate what it is to stand in the sun."

Shaun Hick

CHAPTER THIRTEEN

MOM HAS STAGE FOUR CANCER?

Dad announced to the family that mom was in the fourth stage of Cancer in 2008. It was so emotional for me and I became teary eyed while he told us. I didn't want to believe it but I was hearing it from my dad's own mouth. I felt like I was the only one feeling this emotion. I thought I should be strong for the family, but I couldn't hold back my emotions. For the next few years I was in mourning even though mom was still with us. It had an effect on me in my daily life even though no one could tell. I lost my motivation and drive in my business even though I was still doing it. I was drifting through life and didn't have any aim in my business except my escape when writing. What would I do without my mother? I thought right then I could come over and talk to her anytime I wanted but soon that will be over. The reality of caring for the elderly really hit home with me when I watched mom's battle with stage four Cancer over 4-5 years, come to a sudden halt. After having a stroke, she fell in the bath tub and laid on the floor until my dad and nephew came home and found her lying there.

As I traveled in the ambulance with my mom, even though I have faith, deep down, I thought that this was the end of my mother's life. As I looked into her eyes traveling to the hospital, she continued to look into mine. I could see that she wanted to communicate but couldn't speak. I was with her as she was admitted, while my brothers and sister made their way to the hospital to see her. They did all kinds of test on my mom and all we could do was comfort each other and pray. Even though mom was released after a few days, I knew this was the beginning of the last transition in her life. I've heard about this from many people, but to witness it first hand with your own mother is very terrifying. Even with the cancer, my mom was walking around normally while taking chemo each week. Some days she felt fine and even though she experienced much pain from the cancer she didn't complain. Mom had a bad smoking habit but, it never stopped her from working out and taking her supplements. And she loved reading her health magazines, health newsletters and watching Dr. Oz

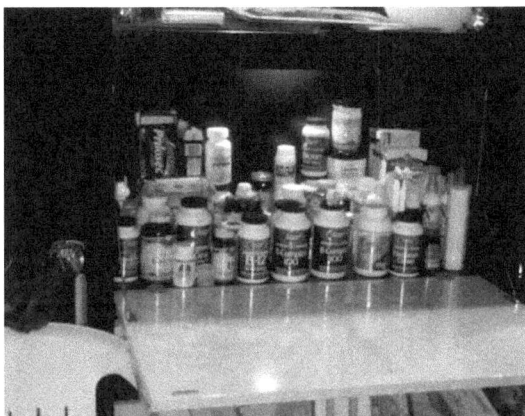

Mom had dad's vitamins in order for him to take everyday

PICTURES OF MOM

Time is the only comforter for the loss of a mother.
Jane Welsh Carlyle

CHAPTER FOURTEEN

MOM'S GONE

As time passed, very fast I saw mom lie in the family home where we grew up. All her life, she was active in the gym and she was a very strong woman. Every day, mom held onto her little rubber ball. She would exercise her hand with the rubber ball as if she could exercise her way back to health. But I know she was tired of fighting. She probably knew it was her time. Me and my brother Joe helped her out of the bed two times in the last two months of her life as my dad stood by her side and took care of her. One of the last highlights of her life was at a family barbeque in the back yard where she accepted the Lord as her personal Savior. My brother Jerry, who is my pastor, is very straight forward. He knew mom didn't have long to live and he wanted to make sure she was ready. He asked her if she was ready to receive the Lord as her personal savior and she started crying. In the family back yard she said her prayer of confession and was a born again a believer.

Transitions can last a long time, but I knew mom didn't want hers to last that long. Mom had taken care of patients all her life and didn't want to be in this situation long. I believe that she thought more about my dad having to take care of her. As I experienced this life changing experience, I wrote an article entitled, "We're all dying; some faster some slower." The last week or so, mom stopped eating and drinking; I knew it would be only a matter of days. I told her I was going to finish my book and dedicate it to her, and I told her how much I loved her.

~~

Dad has to go on without mother

"Jeff, she's gone, Jeff." This was the first time I've ever heard my father cry. I was there in less than ten minutes to comfort my dad. My brothers and sisters came shortly after and dad had to call hospice care. As we came together, we gathered around my mom lying in the bed. We held hands, prayed, praised, worshipped and thanked God, for my mom's life. We were all at peace and we knew that mom was in a better place with no more pain. As the hearse pulled up to take mom to the funeral home, we stood there watching mom's body being taken out of the house. The reality of death hit me. Even though we don't like to mention or talk about it, this will be everyone's last transition. As my siblings and I stood in the drive way to watch our mom take the last ride she would ever take, tears streamed down my face.

~∽~

We have to clear out mom's stuff

A month later, we had to start getting rid of some of mom's things. I knew that it was really hard for dad, but it had to be done. Dad had to cope with living the rest of his life without his wife. It's a transition for him. It's been a huge adjustment and I see that it has change dad's motivation level in certain things. Dad has been a local photographer in Amityville for over forty years. He's taken all types historical pictures for events, including the firehouse, police stations, local events, election events and churches. Everyone knows my dad, but he's slowed down after mom passed. He doesn't go to everything like he used to when mom was alive. Sometimes I forget that dad is also getting up there in age and I know one day we may have to care for him. It's been over two and a half years since my mom has passed and the other day I was at dad's house and he called out her name, "Cass" he said. I came out the bathroom and asked him, "Dad, did you just call mom?" He said, "Yes" and as I left I thought about the adjustment that dad is still making.

I told my younger sister Hope, what I heard and she said, "I was waiting for that." I didn't really make a comment on what she said. They were on their way out so I said, "Alright I'll see you guy's. Have a goodnight" and I left. After the loss of a loved one there is a grieving and mourning period and this process is different for many people. I can't imagine being with someone for over fifty years and then losing them. It may be similar to going through a divorce but since I haven't experienced both I can't tell you. One thing that I do know is we all go through transition. I've gone through many transitions in my life and it won't stop until I'm gone. We'll all have many transitions, some by choice and others by chance. Whether choice or chance it's up to us how we will respond in that moment and sometimes we'll feel all alone. Trust God through it all because he is the master of transition. If you prepare you'll be ready to downsize before transition with less stress, frustration and overwhelm.

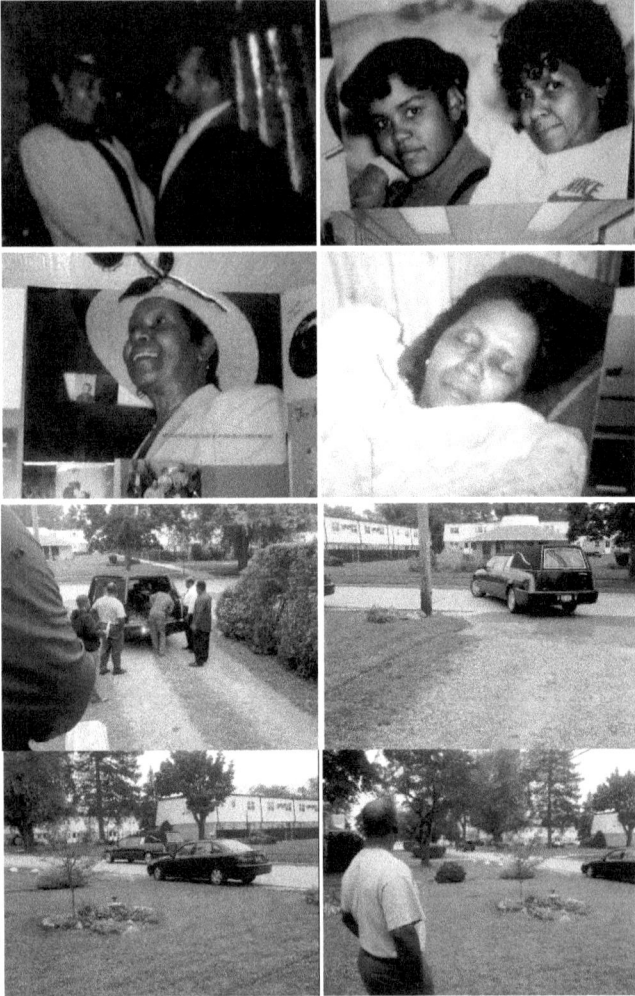

I love you mother

ALARMING STATISTICS FOR THE ELDERLY IN THE US

"By age 80, adults are far more likely to have disabilities than to live in accessible homes."
US CENSUS BUREAU

CHAPTER FIFTEEN

7 THINGS YOU CAN DO TO ELIMINATE STRESS, FRUSTRATION & FEELING OVERWHELMED WHEN TRANSITIONING

1. **Preparing mentally for the transition** will be the most important step in the process of moving. Accept the transition, and move smoothly into this next step in your life. Talk to your family members and research your different options you and your family can make. Don't fight the process. It is natural for this to happen in all of our lives.

2. **Start getting rid of excess clutter** before you have to move. When you wait to move everything at one time it can be very overwhelming if you're not in the right frame of mind. One reason why I don't have a lot of clutter is because every time I moved, I got rid of stuff I wasn't keeping. Remember that most people have way too much stuff that takes up their time, space or energy.

3. **Get the help of a professional** moving manager. There is a growing community of move managers that help seniors transition that makes life easier. I would suggest finding one they'll help you sort, pack and make decisions on important things to keep or toss. They network with movers, downsizing companies that can get rid of the stuff, donation centers, realtors and anyone else that may be of assistance to you.

4. **Prepare for the move** so that you're in the mindset to get rid of stuff. If you're moving to a smaller place you won't be able to fit everything so start to think downsizing. Large multi-million dollar companies do it all the time and it works.

5. **Start over with subtraction** because it's a new chapter for you. Less is more. When you move into your new place, you won't even miss the stuff you haven't seen for years.

6. **Start sorting important documents** before it's time to move, because it will give you plenty of time to locate, organize and shred papers you wouldn't want anyone else to see. This one thing will help eliminate stress when moving because it gives you plenty of time to deal with the important papers in your life.

7. **Contact your local charities** and schedule a time for them to come out and take a look at furniture and other items you may want to give away before the moving process. When you start this process before you have to move it will be more controlled and step by step which makes things much simpler.

ALARMING STATISTICS FOR THE ELDERLY IN THE US

"With the aging of the large baby-boom generation and increased longevity, the 50-and-over population is projected to increase about 20 percent by 2030, to 132 million."
Harvard Joint Center for Housing Studies and AARP Foundation

CHAPTER SIXTEEN

SENIOR DOWNSIZING CHECKLIST

Two Months before Move

- Be patient and don't overwhelm your parent with too much to do
- Contact assisted living center or nursing home and get information
- Contact a senior move manager to assist with the move. They can help with moving arrangements, packing, and setting up in new home.
- Sort through belongings to reduce what will be moved
- Sell or donate items no longer needed
- Contact a clutter removal company to get rid of items left after move or before move which ever you choose
- Get three estimates for move; reserve the movers
- Packing supplies: boxes, tape, markers, scissors and packing material
- Have legal, medical, financial and insurance records accessible

- Contact an elder law attorney to get advice about power of attorney's
- Contact a local realtor or investor

One Month before Move

- Pack items not being used: decorations, seasonal clothing, etc. or arrange for someone to help with the pack
- Make arrangements for pets
- Cancel insurance policies that no longer apply
- Change of address to Post Office

Two Weeks before Move

- Notify Utility companies of the move
- Sign up for services at the new location: cable and/or phone
- Contact a clutter removal company to get rid of items left after move or before move which ever you choose

One Week before Move

- Pack a survival kit of clothes, medicines, special foods to carry through the day after the move
- Finish packing; leave aside items needed in the final week
- Notify magazine, friends, banks, newspaper, service providers bills of new address and phone number

Day before Move

- Prepare parent for move
- Have a supply of packing materials
  - Mark all boxes with room they should go to in new home

Moving Day

- Information to have: phone and cable numbers, movers' number
- Home sale and agent details
- Payment for movers
- At new location walk movers through home and identify the rooms as marked on boxes and where furniture is to be placed
- Have parent stay with sibling or friend during the move day
- Valuable items should remain in a secure place
- Save all moving receipts for possible tax deduction

Parent Move in Day

- Arrive with your parent before a meal
- Tour the new home with parent
- Give parent phone and television directions

Within the First Week of New Home

- Take your parent on a drive around the new home so as to orient to the neighborhood

- Confirm with parent that the new home is set up safely as well as comfortable
- Be open to calls from parent as the adjustment is taking place
- Commit to regular phone calls and visits with your parent so there is a routine to look forward to
- Know the staff and speak to them every visit

The private sector is developing new housing options, technologies and services in recognition of the potential market for assisting older adults with aging in the community.

Harvard Joint Center for Housing Studies

CHAPTER SEVENTEEN

RESOURCES FOR SENIORS

NASMM/ www.Nasmm.com- National association of senior move manages/Assisting seniors in transition

NAELA/ www.Naela.com- National Academy of Elder Law Attorney's/ Elder law information you need to stay current

Sun Suffolk/ www.Seniorumbrella.com- The Senior Umbrella Network offers monthly networking opportunities for professionals serving seniors

AARP www.aarp.org/aarp-foundation- AARP Foundation helps millions of struggling older adults 50 and over win back opportunity

SRA Senior Resource Alliance- http://www.seniorresourcealliance.org- Helping find the information, resources and services seniors need

SCB/ www.seniorcitizensbureau.com Resource for the elderly, children of the elderly, other caregivers, advocates and professionals!

Online Directory and resource guide that lists various housing, product and service providers! National hotline! The seniority hotline, available 24 hours a day, 7 days a week for senior members and those with vision limitations.

Assistance to Caregivers! Information for the senior's and continuing education and networking opportunities for the senior community and Industry as a whole!

Long Island Transitions: Kathleen Mazza
Senior move manager

www.Seniorserviceassistants.com
Judy Torre

Monthly Newsletters:
___Yes Jeff I want to Sign up for Two
FREE month of your monthly newsletters:
I understand when I sign up online I'll get
a copy of Downsizing before Transition for
$6.97 cents + shipping to share with a
friend!

~~~

*Visit the websites below and sign up for the newsletter
you are interested in*

Downsizing before Transition: How senior's
transition with Less Stress Frustration and
Overwhelm
www.DownsizingbeforeTransition.com

Creating Dreams 4 Youth: The Secret To
Creating Your Own Job With a Fast Growing
Company with Plenty Of Room For
Advancement In The New Economy
www.CreatingDreams4youth.com

Contact Info:
> Jeff Turner
> PO Box 816
> Amityville NY 11701
> 631-417-2022

jeffturnerjeff@gmail.com
www.jeffturnertalksjunk.com / Blog
www.DownsizingbeforeTransition.com: Senior transition without the stress frustration & overwhelm

CreatingDreams4Youth.org: Young people job creation on demand

Coming this spring: May 11 2015
"Look Mom I Finally Cleaned My Room!"
Mom's simple success principle… Get rid of the clutter!

Coming this fall: Sept 26th 2015
"Start with Subtraction!"
How Anyone Can Be Super Successful In Business & Life Starting With Subtraction

ALARMING STATISTICS FOR THE ELDERLY IN THE US

"By age 85 more than two-thirds of individuals have some type of disability no matter what their race/ethnicity, income, or housing tenure."
AARP Foundation

ABOUT THE AUTHOR

Jeff Turner first cleaned out a house at age ten with his dad and brothers. He started his own junk removal business about thirty years later. Jeff noticed many people had way too much stuff! He studied many years of business and marketing on his own.

He knew in order to stand out in his industry he needed to be different. He started this by subtracting. He removed the word junk from his message (Instead he called it clutter), and he stopped targeting the main junk removal market. He started targeting seniors in transition by referral, he gives stuff away to people in need, he sells stuff and lets his clients know they are indirectly part of a mission to create jobs and opportunities for young people. He understands people would rather know their stuff is being used, and not just dumped for garbage.

www.ingramcontent.com/pod-product-compliance
Lightning Source LLC
LaVergne TN
LVHW051353080426
835509LV00020BB/3416